COPYRIGHT

These Poems are of my own hand.

They have been published on several poetry websites before being collated for this collection.

Some have been amended slightly, grammar changes and some have been shortened as the ending was not appropriate for this collection.

No part of this book may be reproduced, stored in a retrieval system or transmitted by any means without the written permission of the Author Jacqueline Mead.

I have permission for the use of all photos in this book, they are either my own or under license from Adobe Stock Photos.

Because of the dynamic nature of the internet, some links contained in this book may change overtime and may no longer be available.

I am a Poet who enjoys writing about the Environment and
Nature. As I have only been writing since 2017, none of the Poems
in this book are older than a couple of years.
I have brought them together for this collection. I am an observer
and I write what I see and how it makes me feel at the time.

What inspires me the most about Nature is the beauty found in the
smallest of things. Beauty they say is in the eye of the beholder
and that is true in all walks of nature. Personally, I find beauty in
Sunsets, Fields of Green and Park Benches as I hope this collection
of Poems illustrates. There is a great variety and you will find
some that have been written about Africa for an African poetry
website I belong to, inspiration coming from a video of how
children make their way to school.

To me Nature doesn't just mean Flowers and Birds. Nature is
found in the ebb and flow of a river how it meanders to its final
destination, the changes of the season, a Full Moon.

If you already know of my Poems you will notice that some of
them have changed, I have made grammatical changes to some
and removed the endings of others.

I hope you enjoy the Poems please feel free to contact me.

E: Author@jacquelinemead.com

or visit my website

W: www.jacquelinemead.com

You can also find me on Poetry websites
www.realisticpoetry.com and www.hellopoetry.com

Or on Social Media
Facebook: @JacquelineMeadAuthor
Twitter: @jackiem158
Instagram: @jackiespoetrypage

INDEX OF POEMS

Life of a Slug

I don't live life in the fast lane; being a Slug.
I am one of nature's slowest moving insect or bug.

I take all day getting from A to B.
On the lookout for shiny green leaves; for my tea.

Gardeners dislike me, they lay down a blue pill.
The intention to make me very ill.

I will have the last laugh, with them yet.
As their beloved Son, covets me for his Pet.

Gladly I live to see another day; nowhere to go, nothing
much to say.

Moving slowly from A to B; leaving a trail behind me,
silvery and slimy.

Living life slowly and cautiously, and that suits me.

The Life of a Bee

Busy, busy
Buzzing, buzzing, buzzing
Worker Bee, Queen Bee, Bumblebees, Honeybees
Harvesting, pollinating, nesting
Producing Wax and Honey
The productive Life of a Bee

Sid the Snake

Sid the Snake, slithers
Sid the Snake, stealthily glides
Amongst rushes, Sid the Snake hides

Venom in his Fangs
Sid the Snake, hunts for its prey
Will Sid the Snake eat today

Sid hisses his warning
Fangs immobilise, cause pain
Sid the Snake, winning today

Avoid Sid the Snake
Give Sid the Snake a wide berth
Stay safe, know your worth

Sid the Snake, slithers
Sid the Snake, stealthily glides
Amongst rushes, Sid the Snake hides

The Life of a Butterfly

I am a thing of beauty, a sight to behold.
I extend my wings to fly and hover, when I grow tired, they
fold.

I am the Red Admiral variety.
on top my colours are black wings, orange
bands and spots of white.
Underneath my colours are of a different sight.

From early spring to winter I can be found in
woodlands of the south.
Laying my larvae on nettles, drinking from flowers beautiful
mouths.

I start my life as larvae, transform into a chrysalis from which my
adult body grows.

Fatherless and motherless I make my own way in this world.
once metamorphosis is complete, my wings I unfurl.

I flap my wings and fly from flower to flower pollinating,
as I go.
One of nature's own miracles.

Daffodils

Dew topped yellow flowers
Appear vibrant,
Fragrant and
Full of hope that Spring is here.

Ornate, tall, long green stems
Decorating our roads, river ways, fields and, hills
Inspirational sight as they appear clustered in groups
Looking delightful as they display a kaleidoscopic array
Spring has definitely sprung

Rainy Days

How do you spend Rainy Days?
Does your mind fall into a foggy haze?
Do you go back to bed, snuggle under the duvet?
Does your partner make it a sweet duet?

Do you indulge yourself with a Hot chocolate, pile it high
with marshmallows?
Sip it slowly, allow yourself to melt, mellow.

Do you settle down in front of the T. V.?
Watching reruns, making a little time for me?

OR

Do you embrace the rain on your face?
Put on your wellies, splash in puddles?
Not caring if your clothes get in a muddle.
Rejuvenating yourself with laughter?
Chasing rainbows and your happy ever after.

Make Rainy Days lots of fun.
Sunny Days follow and by their nature bring the Sun.

The Hunter

A Lion called Leo, that's his name.
Golden Fleece body and a head framed with a golden mane.
Leo is King of all he surveys.
As he stretches his body and basks in the rays, of the midday
sun of the Savannah Plains.

Leo is the head of the pride.
The Alpha Male to the Lioness bride.
Father to seven newly born cubs.
He sits alone, camouflaged amongst the scrub.

Leo senses a danger ahead.
He pricks up his ears and lifts his head.
Sensing trouble ahead, he sets loose a loud roar.
Scarring the Vultures, who overhead soar.

The Lioness hears the warning sound.
Gathers her cubs and ushers them to the ground.
Lion and Lioness, now working as a Team.
Lion and Lioness, one skilled fighting machine.

The Lion starts prowling, picking up pace.
Keeping himself hidden behind rushes, not leaving a trace.
The Lioness stands proud and alert.
Eager that no cub should get hurt.

The Lion continues hunting its prey.
Stealthily circling and closing in upon his catch.
The preyed will not see another day.
Leo uses his large claws to trap, snatch and dispatch.

Lion and Lioness, a winning team
Nature's skilled fighting machine.

Not hunting for a thrill
This is hunting for survival, kill or be killed.

The Lion returns to his place under the sun.
Once again basking in the rays.
His Lioness and cubs safe for another day.

You make your way to School

You make your way to school, any way you can
Avoiding deadly insects, crossing barren, unfriendly wasteland

You travel on broken boats, scooping water by hand as you go
Riding ponies across the cold and frozen snow
You use your hands to climb the mountain to the top
There is no obstacle put in your way that will make you stop

I salute you, your strength and bravery you show every day
A child in body but mature in every other way
The price of an education, is any price too high to pay?
In ten years, you will be educated, learned
Grown up in body, you will no longer be a kid

Use your knowledge wisely, give back to your people where you
can
Welcome to the world all your efforts have contributed to making
you a full grown and equal Human

Lillies

Slowly, opening, displaying their leaves
Through hues of all colours their magic weaves

Calla, Tiger, Stargazer
Fragrant, Vibrant, Bright as a lazer

Sitting pretty, on my kitchen shelf
Water maintaining their perfect health

Purple in colour they are very pleasing to the eye
Everyone comments as they pass by

A wonderful fragrance perfumes the room
A wonderful flower, a beautiful bloom

The perfect flower to say "thank you"
Or to walk down the aisle with, when you say "I do

Man's Best Friend

The Dog they say is Man's Best Friend.
Loyal and faithful, he will follow his Master until the Worlds End.
He runs, he lays, he sits on command.
If his Master requests he will lay his paw in his hand.

Man's Best Friend comes in all shapes and sizes.
Some are bouncy, fun and full of surprises,
Some are as fast as a streak of lightening,
Some are quite big and to small children quite frightening,
Some will gladly retrieve the ball, place it at your feet,
Some will only obey your command, for a small treat.

Man's Best Friend, many types abound.
Some have short bodies, with bellies that touch the ground,
Some are so hairy you can't see their eyes,
Some are so small they look undersize,
Some are large and quite clumsy,
Some are yappy and some are grumpy.

Man's Best Friend work hard for their Masters.
They carry out tasks that really matter,
They listen out for the doorbell to ring,
Bark when the boiling kettle sings,
They guide their Master when out for a walk,
Sit obediently at your feet when you stop to talk.

Man's Best Friend is a beloved member of the family.
Makes himself at home, takes the best seat in the house, happily.

The family wouldn't have it any other way,

One thing is for sure, Man's Best Friend is here to stay.

Sunrise at 39,000 feet

Wow how privileged am I?
To be 39,000 feet high
And witness the Sun rise

The Sky awash with colours of red, orange and Gold
This is art at its best
Nothing else can attest
As we watch the day start to unfold

First the sky is painted many colours
Then the Sun, a dark rust, pokes its head above the clouds
A perfect round face sits proud
Surveying the land from its perch up high
A royalty, of sorts, in the Sky

This is natural beauty
Mother Nature flaunting her booty
As the Lady says welcome to another day

White Sand, Golden Sun, Blue Seas

White Sands, Golden Sun, Blue Seas

White sands, golden sun in the sky, warm blue sea
All that is needed to revive me

Swimming, snorkeling, walking and talking
A soft hand in mine
A glass of sweet red wine

White sands, golden sun in the sky, warm blue sea
All that is needed to revive me

A romantic meal for two on the sand
A hot night with my Man

White sands, golden sun in the sky, warm blue sea
All that is needed to revive me

At dusk the sunsets painting the sky; as it says its goodbye for the
night
Such a wondrous, glorious sight

White sands, golden sun in the sky, warm blue sea
All that is needed to revive me

An adventure at sea
Hunting for Sharks
My hubby and me
Up with the Larks
Throwing buckets of fish overboard
Repaid with not one but many
A dazzling reward
White sands, golden sun in the sky, warm blue sea

All that is needed to revive me

Dolphins in the Indian Ocean Sea
Pods swimming, leaping having fun
Basking in the warm midday sun

White sands, golden sun in the sky, warm blue sea
All that is needed to revive me

Seared into my memories; my holiday in the Maldives
White sands, golden sun in the sky, warm blue sea
All that is needed to revive me

Summer Rain

Summer Rain falling
Lowering warmth of the day
Nourishing the Land
Reviving life in our plants
Summer Rain, falling again

Summer Rain falling
Keep an umbrella on hand
Coats optional choice
Summer Rain nourishes land
We run around dodging drops

Summer Rain falling
Dark clouds full of Summer Rain
Falling on flood plains
Causing panic and distress
As the rain blows through again

<u>Clouds</u>

Grey clouds gathering
The day becoming colder
This is our Summer
British Summertime over?
Here's wishing that Summer stays

Beautiful Day

The heat beats, upon the ground
I feel it is going to be a beautiful day
As I welcome the warmth of the Sun's rays

The Suns power; to illuminate all around
Flowers tilt their heads to the sky, in worship of the growth
the Sun brings
Birds flying in the sky, rejoicing, sweetly sing

The warmth the Sun generates, brings a smile to one's eyes
It stays there a while, welcoming people passing by

As children play by the Sea, making new friends
Gardeners in their gardens, flowers and plants they tend

Yesterday was the day of Rain
Today brings the Sun and Summer in a day, again

Daisies

Daisies a flash of white in a field of green
One of the most beautiful sights you ever will see
The daisy spreads itself far and wide
Vastly covering the countryside
Butterflies and Bees hover by
You even attract the common fly
Strength in numbers, you grow and give;
Your nectar for other insects to live
The Daisies wanting nothing in return
They just ask you show some discern
As your child runs through the fields; making daisy chains
Ensure when they leave, some daisies remain

A Day in the Lake District

With my husband by my side I sit and reflect
Upon my image in the stream
At wonder in the changes of my being
The weather warm but windy, with oft a gentle spray of rain
I feel lively, lightness appears to be my gain

Sat at a spot of such beauty, it takes your breath away
Appreciating the silence, as you give thanks for the day
In front of you great Lakes of Water some world famous
being sailed or swam side to side
Behind you in contrast high Peaks and Mountains, waiting
to be climbed

There are paths to be walked, Roman Forts to be found
Cruises to be taken, bikes to ride, hidden gems all around
Ice creams to be bought, footsteps to be walked
Pubs, Cafes and Restaurants by the Water sought
There is history to be lived amongst the many Villages
There is romance to be read in Poetry of old
Wordsworth, Coleridge and Southey Poets of pure gold
Their stories and Poems, their legacies, forever being told

There is a bench ...

There is a bench; appeared upon the banks of the canal
It looks a little bit rough and a little banal
It is not dedicated with a bronze plaque
It is simply decorated with that of the River Exe's track

It has no lack of customers wishing to take a seat
Students on their way home, take a moment browsing on
their phone
Elderly people bring take away fish and chips instead of
taking them home
I've seen people pick up speed, quicken their pace
So as to keep a seat for them and not lose their place
Children playing on their bikes on the grass around
Their Mum and Dads laying a picnic on the ground

It has brought much happiness to our lovely green space
Creating memories for people who are making it their go-to
place
Let us say nothing of its appearance and embrace the good
That some clever person has crafted out of a chunk of wood

As I was walking along the bank of the Canal

As I was walking along the bank of the Canal, fog covering the
ground like a cloak.
I thought I heard the jolly sound of a Frog croak.
The Canal usually bright blue of colour.
Cast an unusually dark eerie, discolour.
I carried on walking towards St David's Station, my destination
Whilst composing a Poem with my imagination.
In front, I could not see more than 10feet ahead.
But I swear a saw the wings of an albatross, overhead.

To the left as I walked beside green open fields, I suddenly heard
the sound of a Swan squeal.
To my right, the Canal cast a dark and dreary backdrop.
The banks of the Canal usually lined with trees; you could barely
see their tops.

Fifteen minutes in and I began to feel the warmth of the sun, hitting
my heels.
The path ahead lit by the warm soft glow of the sun, giving the start
of the day an ethereal feel.
Twenty minutes and now the fog begins to lift My spirits are
beginning to change, uplift.

Twenty-five minutes have now gone by and I have almost arrived,
it usually takes me twenty-three.
The fog has lifted and now I can see, exactly was happening around,
I could see people walking their dogs, walkers walking and runners'
jog.
The trees on the banks of the Canal have burst through the fog.

I could see People at the start of their day, some stop you and say,
"good morning what a nice day".
Some just smile as you pass them, on your way.

Some pass you by, phones to their ears, never catching your eye.
Some smile sweetly, a little shy.

When the fog lifts and the Sun cast its rays.
You hope it's going to be the start of a beautiful day.
Hope grows therein.
Hope for better, warm days, beautiful spring flower displays.
The hope for warm sunny days begins.

A Child of Africa

A child of Africa
A land of colour and spice
A child of Africa
Brought up on the flavours of paprika and rice

Dreaming of becoming a Doctor or Nurse
No money for education leftover in the purse
Though the African child is able
Mother and Father working hard to put food on the table

A child of Africa
A land of colour and spice
A child of Africa
Brought up on the flavours of paprika and rice

Every child deserves the chance to achieve their dreams
Become Engineers, Politicians, a child Prodigy
Become the Captain of their destiny
Be given the opportunity to succeed, raise their self esteem

A child of Africa
A land of colour and spice
A child of Africa
Brought up on the flavours of paprika and rice

Every child deserves the opportunity to shine
Aspiring to be their best self
Realising their dreams, not leaving them behind on the shelf

A child of Africa
A land of colour and spice
A child of Africa
Brought up on the flavours of paprika and rice

A Child of Africa, daydreaming
Of being set free from the shackles of poverty
Aspiring to be a leader, created out of Liberty

A child of Africa
A land of colour and spice
A child of Africa
Brought up on the flavours of paprika and rice

The African child sits under the Sun
Knowing they are equal to everyone
Not cast aside by colour or race
They are educated, have freedom and space
To explore their dreams, succeed
To be a creator and by example Lead

Pelicans and Iguanas

Pelicans gracefully sweep and soar in the clear blue Caribbean sky.
Iguanas lazy at first, quicken as they walk by.

Pelicans hunting for their tea, hover over the green blue Caribbean
sea.
Iguanas of brown, blue and green, disguise themselves, not keen to
be seen.

Pelicans, hover, swoop then dive, catching fish for their tea.
Showing their skills to anyone that wishes to see.
Wonderful birds in all their glory.

Iguanas flick out their tongue to catch a leaf for their tea.
Avoiding the rays of the hot sun, underneath a shady tree.

Fascinating to watch and see these beautiful creatures in all their
glory.

A single leaf...

falls to the ground
It's colour is a standout yellow in a carpet of brown
This leaf represents life not yet complete
Still resplendent in colour as it falls at your feet
Life not over still holding on
Life to be cherished for however long

Aruban Sunset

As the sun sets on another glorious day.
All the colours of fire, come out to play.
Red, yellow and orange light up the sky.
Creating patterns to delight your eye.
Sitting, relaxing, drink in hand.
As the sunsets on these gorgeous sands.

Clouds #2

Clouds you stealthily pass us by.
To where I wonder and know not why.
You quietly move with little noise but lots of grace.
Moving at ease throughout the vast space.
Sometimes you are grey and heavy with rain.
Then you release the water and flood our drains.
Sometimes you are light, fluffy and white.
Combined with an early morning sun and you are quite the
sight.
Your form creates patterns in the bright blue sky.
Visible on earth to the human eye.
It is quite breathtaking and makes me smile.
Light, fluffy and white clouds, please hang around for a
while.

Autumn

Autumn, I love this time of year
Not quite Winter and still some sunny days
But the leaves they are a turning
Changing colours from green to red, yellow and brown
Trees shredding their leaves all about you on the ground
Autumn, I love this time year

Colours of Spring

I walk the river down one side and travel back the other.
I watch the people walk their dogs and children with their mother.
I see the beauty along the course, birds nesting in the trees,
swans swimming with their young,
the fast running water of the weir,
the blueness of the sky,
the yellowness of the sun.
I see the colours of the earth, surrounding us in nearby fields,
where farmers have ploughed the soil the colour is earthly brown.
The field next to it is a blaze of green,
what the brown field will yield is yet to be seen.
Flowers starting to open their colourful heads, Daffodils, Primroses,
Tulips , Bluebells Snowdrops, Crocuses and Hyacinths, in various
shades, of Yellow, Red, Blue and White, it really is a beautiful sight.
The warmth of Spring starting to generate various shades of Red,
Blue, White, Yellow and Green
The palette of Spring is a riot of colour and truly wonderful to see

Changes of the Season

Seasons they come and go
Winter is long and cold
Log fires burning to warm your bones
Children singing carols in front of altars
Chestnuts cooked over open fires
Christmas Day comes then into New Year, slowly bringing
optimism and cheer for the following year

Slowly Winter changes to Spring
Eternally hopeful with all that it brings
Lambs being born in open fields
Cattle outdoors grazing, milk and beef is their yield
Flowers starting to open up, daffodils, tulips, and buttercups
Brightening the landscape for all to see, days warming up
nicely

Along comes summer
The sun is strong and days last ten hours long,
Children have no summer school, playing outdoors is the
rule, splashing in pools, playing in the park, allowed to stay
out until almost dark
Barbeques in the garden with friends and family, day trips
to the beach and splashing in the sea.

Slowly, slowly the season changes to Autumn
Leaves change colours, dropping to the floor
Animals go in hibernation finding safe places to store; food
for them and their young
Now the days are shorter we don't see much sun
Days shortening, darkness ascending upon us all too soon as
the sun disappears to be replaced by the moon.

Ebb and Flow

The River Exe flexes and flows, as the water meanders sometimes fast and sometimes slow.

It opens its arms and stretches wide, wriggles its toes and opens its eyes, to greet a brand new day.

It glistens and gleams on a bright sunny day as it tumbles slowly from A to B, everyone smiling at how it flows so freely, making them stop and take some time, helping them find peace, become free of mind.

On an overcast day it appears angry and dark, it sounds so loud, like thunder it roars, making each of us aware of its presence, it can bring down trees and power cables, making us feel very unstable.

The rains fall heavy and the River Table rises, we have done our maths there are no surprises, we have built Canals, Reservoirs and Weirs to contain the extra additional fallen rain.

Still this may not be enough, the River Bank is Mr Tough, it will burst its banks without a care, leaving us in its wake, no prisoners it will take.

But the path it flows is luscious and green, it's a beautiful spot very serene, birds and fish swim in its waters, flowers and trees grow by its side, adults and children play in kayaks and canoes, it's somewhere to go where there are lots of things to do.

As the River Exe Ebbs and Flows sometimes fast and sometimes slow, mimicking the pace of life, sometimes fast and sometimes slow, we all need a place to go, where we can feel peace of mind, relax, sit back and unwind - where do you go to find your peace of mind?

Ever Changing Landscape

Autumnal colours vibrant and strong.
Framing the Landscape, broad and long.
Trees of different type and colour.
Various combinations to discover.
Leaves of Red, Orange, Yellow, Brown and Green.
Combining to create a wonderfully, warming scene.
Deciduous trees, shedding their leaves.
Decorating the floor, treasures left for children to explore.
The days darken, the heat lessens, the wind and rain set in.
This can only mean one thing, Winter is keen to begin.

If I were an Island

I would hold out my hand
Five fingers all covered in soft white sand
Wash you in bright blue seas
Kiss you with golden sun
Add a sprinkle of cafe and bars for fun

I would caress your cheeks with a light wind or two
I would care for your spirit by offering adventurous
activities to do

I would sing beautiful music to your ears
Make the island safe and happy to chase away your fears
I would add some wildlife a rugged coastline too, maybe
even a petting zoo.

I would most of all build a home off the beaten track,
so we can get lost, no way of finding our way back

Images of Summer

Blue skies, Daily highs
Green fields
Keeping it real
Soft sand, Hand in hand
Yellow sun, Days just begun
Rainy days, Foggy haze
Orange sun
Skies ablaze
Softly lapping seas
At your feet they tease
Large crashing waves
Wiping you off your feet, quick save
Rock pools on the shore
Children climbing to explore
Sandcastles on the beach
Waves just out of reach
Yellow flowers
Pollen power
Temperature 28 degrees
Some people with hay fever, attempting not to sneeze
Kites flying in the sky
Children laughing nearby
Picnics spread upon the ground
Variety of flavours abound
Swans swimming in the lake
Cygnets fighting for breadcrumbs to take
Dogs running in the park
Owners chasing them, not to bark
Cricket playing in the field
"Not out, surely" "umpire what do you feel"?
Sitting out on the decking
Last of the sun's rays savouring
Bright Full Moon
The end of the day has come too soon

O Little Bird

O little bird, perched high up in the tree
Come flap your wings, fly down, converse with me

O little bird come perch upon my arm
I will ensure that your tiny being comes to no harm

O little bird, you tweet your tuneful song all day long, loud
and clear
Come whisper sweet nothings in my ear

O little bird perched high up in the tree
Flap your wings, fly little bird, be free, be free

Snow

Fall snow fall
Cover the ground in white as far as you can see
We don't get you very often, but you are beautiful to see
Fall snow fall

Strong Winds

The doors are wide open
The sky is blue
The wind is cold it cuts right through
I love the wind upon my face
It reminds me to embrace what is on its way
Who knows what will come
with every day

I love the wind blowing through the house
It sweeps the air and makes it pure
Pure crisp air for all to breathe
It's done its job, it may now leave

It swirls and whirls and with it takes
Memories some new and some untold
But it never takes the old ones that are valuable to you
The wind leaves them behind for you to cherish once it's gone

Who knew the wind could be so strong?

Sunset

When I left work tonight at five o'clock
The light was falling but it wasn't dark
It was as though Van Gogh had taken his brush
Painted the sky in a faint blush
All different hues from grey to white to red and blue
And it got me thinking of you
I wish I could have captured its sight and shared it with you
tonight
You would have loved the picture and the glow
How I still miss you so xx

Sunset #2

The sun sets low behind the trees
The sight of it bringing you to your knees
The trees branches still bare of leaves
Gives the sky a hauntingly beautiful glow
And your thankful to have been there to see the sunset
beneath the trees
To be brought to your knees by the outstanding beauty
that's nature

Sunset #3

The sky burned orange, like a fire
When the sun goes then comes the darkest hour

The beauty of Nature

Nature is a wonder and joy
From tiny creatures to giant beasts
Weather storms from the East
Geysers ready to blow
Snails moving very slow

From microscopic bugs to giant turtles on the beach
Birds flying high and out of reach
Rainbows and Sunsets with bright red skies
Super blue blood Moons and northern lights
Sloths idly lazing in a tree
Bees, butterflies moths and flies pollinating flowers as they
fly by
Elephants and rhinoceros drinking at the watering hole
Worms that are bright giving off a glow
Stars twinkling in the dark night
The sun shining strong and bright

Each creature differs in stripes or spots, tusks or horns,
hooves or paws
Some have poison in their bodies ready to release in a bite
Some are docile creatures keeping their selves hidden from
sight
You have mountain ranges that go on for miles
Painted ladies making you smile
Whales with humpbacks and Sharks with hammerheads
Rivers that give creatures a place to call their bed
Swans that glide effortlessly and with grace
Flightless birds that can sprint and win a race
Monkeys, tigers, crocodiles and kangaroos
Bears brown and black, Polar that are white, Pandas and
Koala too
Roaming plantations not kept caged in zoos

Coral reefs keeping coastlines safe from waves crashing on
the shore
A big wide world for everyone to explore
Waterfalls 1000metres high, water cascading and falling to
the ground
Hydrating the grasses and plants that surround
All of this and more can be found if you open your eyes and
look around
Take stock of the beauty outside your door
Recycle plastics don't drop them on the floor or overboard at
sea, don't fly tip your rubbish selfishly
Plant wildflowers in your garden and you will be repaid by
a very beautiful colours ablaze
Attracting Bees and butterflies to your home
Teaching your children to respect and admire
Keeping the beauty alight and on fire
For future generations to cherish and see
Keeping nature healthy and robust for eternity

The June rain came

One day out walking in the park
It was as if the lights went out; the sky went dark
The rain came and the river levels rose high
I didn't know so much rain could be held by the sky
The rain fell harder it turned to rocks as it fell
The landscape looked as though snow had settled
Covering surfaces white, the hailstones lay
It had been a very unusual day
I reminded myself it was summer; June
Let's hope the sun comes back soon

The Orchid

She sits upon the sill,
Tall, proud and very still
Her colour is delicate, pale like a fine piece of lace
She has a face full of beauty and grace
She does not come every year; we miss her when we're apart
But the time she is with us brings love and joy to our heart

Tranquillity

Before me lies a vastness, it looks much like emptiness
Not within my Heart
Or Upon the ground
It is in the deep blue Indian Ocean; Tranquillity is to be
found

Noiseless, except for the hum of the boat
In the middle of the Indian Ocean, we float
Basking in the hot golden Sun
Watching the Pods of Dolphins, leaping, playful having fun

Life cannot get much better for me
As I float in the middle of the Indian Ocean Sea
I believe I have found my peace, I have found my
tranquillity

Water

Water does it for me, there's nothing I like more than living by the sea.

You live in Exeter I here you cry, that's not by the sea and I agree but it has a river and canal and that's good enough for me.

Water relaxes me, I can watch it roll and tumble all day, watching it go on its merry way.

Water chills me, I solve issues by gazing at the water, suddenly ideas abound as the water makes its way round.

Water brings back happy memories of days spent by the sea. Learning how to surf and eating ice lollies.

When you are an island your inclined to think that we'll never run out of the drink.

However, let's not take water for granted, let's not dare, I want my children and grandchildren to be able to stand and stare.

Waves

Sat on the beach looking out to sea.
Memories in my mind, running free.

The blue sea ebbs and flows.
The white tips of the waves glow.
The sound of the wave is noisy.
The wind is blowing breezy.

The wave begins its inward journey.
Picking up speed, it becomes very loudly.
The wave begins to peak and crest.
The wave looks majestic, at is best.

Its journey nearly over, as it begins to fall.
It has reached its destination and crashes to the shore.

The wave once a thing of beauty is no more.
Its role in life is to live and breathe.
Show people beauty that brings you to your knees.

All day people and children play in the sea, swimming and surfing freely.
But never take the sea for granted be sure you know the rules.
Being unsafe at the seaside is really not cool.

Lost in my memories of beaching days.
There is no better place to be than;

Standing on a beach with your feet in the sea

In the still of the night

In the still of the night
A Pale Moon casts its light
It comes and goes, goes and comes
Like it is playing with us as it safely guides us home

One minute the Moon is there to be seen, in its fullest glory
The next hidden behind a cloud, like it's a character acting
out its own story
The moonlight is just bright enough to guide us home
Letting us know as we walk in the dark that we are not
alone

We walk and talk, holding hands, laughing with our friends
The Moon continues its game of hide and seek, dipping
behind the clouds
It is not long before it's back taking a peep, ensuring our
safe-keep
Guiding us safely home, to our houses in the street, once
there were street lights to guide us home
Now I'm glad to say that conserving energy means you are
honoured to witness nature coming out to play

The Moon tonight is pale and round it looks very small in
the sky and its colour is milky white
The clouds are shades of white and a little bit of grey
I ponder what the clouds will be like tomorrow when the
Moon goes in and the Sun comes out to play
Will the grey in the clouds disappear, giving way to blue
and warmth?
Will they darken every hour resulting in a downpour?

Nature is perfect in everything it does, wrapping its arms
around us all, in one big happy hug

The Swan

The Swan glides effortlessly across the River
The only sign, rings on the water that look as though the
River shivers

Six cygnets by their side
Protecting their young, their eyes cast far and wide
Fear for their young makes them angry
Makes them shriek and shrill
Don't get too close they will bite you with their bill

On a good day though, you will see them, displaying their
feathers magnificently
Wings out wide and neck held high
As they prepare to leave the waters and take to the sky

The Swan so full of grace
You really do enhance our space.

Fall

In New England, a sight; like no other

Created by Natures very own Mother

A sight so dazzling, brightening the Autumnal skies

Creating an exhilarating scene, delighting our eyes

Leaves of many varieties, of strong and vibrant colours

Turning from Green to Yellow, Orange, Red and Brown

Before they slip form the branches and

Laying a coat of many colours down

For us to walk, jump, and run through, upon the ground

Northern Lights

We flew two and half thousand miles to Iceland; bearing the cold
All in the sake of chasing the Aurora Borealis's enchanting glow

The first night, a bit of a disaster, the northern lights would not
come out to play
They hid themselves away shyly, saving themselves for another day
It was late in the season, you may not get to see the lights; people
reasoned.

The next day though the sun was out and the blue skies crystal clear
We knew in our hearts, the Aurora Borealis were very near
We booked ourselves on a Northern Lights chaser
Following reports, and signs of lights in the sky, chasing nature's
laser

Our coach pulled into a field; we were told the lights were near by
Instructed to use our cameras and not our human eye
Flash disabled and lens on slow
We pointed our cameras heavenwards, towards the glow
To the human eye the sky was a milky white
Through the camera you saw the haze of a soft green light
The hazy green light created an ethereal glow;
whilst
Particles and atoms clashing together, sparking, arcing, igniting
creating; their own spectacular fireworks show

A wonderful trip, a lifetime event, I could have stayed forever
To get to see these sights you must make every endeavour
Include the trip on your bucket list, mark it important, one not to
miss!

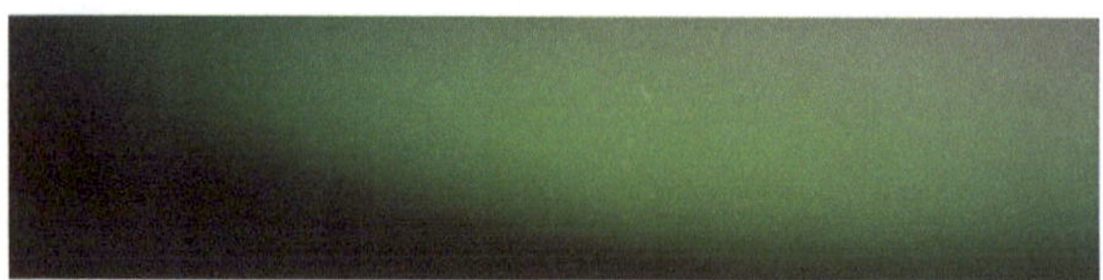

BONUS CONTENT

As well as writing about Nature and the Environment, I love to write Poetic Tales.

I have written several about the same characters a Mouse with a House, a Frog and Bee, An Elf with one Ear and A Fly with one Eye and a Horse and His Master and I have ideas to make a future book out of these.

However I wanted to include a sample of my Poems which tell a story, hint at a moral and are written with fun and humour. Below is Mr Lee the Monkey and Ted the Giraffe and I hope you enjoy.

Mr Lee the Monkey and Ted the Giraffe

There was a young Monkey called Mr Lee
Who loved to hang out, swinging in the trees.

One day suddenly from below, a Giraffes head appeared, real slow
"Hi" he spoke my name is Ted
"I am looking for somewhere to lay my head"
"Not here" replied Mr Lee
"I am afraid there is no room for you in my tree"
"Oh" Ted the Giraffe replied and walked away with a heavy sigh

Mr Lee feeling he had been a bit mean
Offered Ted the Giraffe a leaf so green
Mr Lee said " I am sorry I didn't mean to say, there was nowhere for your head to lay"
"I am swinging from branch to branch, tree to tree, I don't usually have visitors, it's usually only me!"

"That is okay" said Ted "I have found myself a soft hay bed"
"But what you are doing looks like fun, do you fancy
company of another one?"
Mr Lee considered the request, it would be fun to have the
company of another one.
"Yes, indeed" he did reply "although you are rather tall, I
believe your knees would knock on the floor"
"I don't want you to hurt your knees whilst your swinging
in the trees"
"Why don't you walk by my side, we can talk as we cover
the countryside"

Ted the Giraffe was delighted to make a new friend.
And that is very nearly the end.
Just enough time to say have you made a new friend today?
It does not matter how you look, how tall you are or how
you speak
Nobody likes to feel lonely
Take the time, say "hello" boldly
Children are not bound by heavy chains
Make a friend don't refrain
Say "hi" again, again and again